FROM THE SAME SOIL

WE ARE ALIKE TREES AND HUMANS

BY DOROTHY (DOT) HOLMAN

1

Introduction

From the Same Soil

This book is about trees and humans, but it's not to inform you of how many trees are in the world or how many people are in the world. This book is for you to see the trees through my eyes and start to look at trees in a different way. They are everywhere you go in our world like humans. Trees and humans are alike. There are life lessons in the trees, that is what I hope this book will do for you and you will pass this wisdom and knowledge on to friends, family and the next generation. Just be who you are created to be and our lives will be beautiful inside and out.

Dorothy (Dot) Holman

Your donations for this book will help me help others.

PRESENTED TO:

From: Megan

Date: 11/4/24

Remarks Blessings

By Dorothy (Dot) Holman

Dot Holman

Dedication to:

To my daughter Patina Holman, my son Bobby Holman, my grandson Brandon Holman, and my niece Princella Ridley, who have always been there for me. To all the pastors and ministers in my life who have helped me become the woman I am today. To God be the glory.

Acknowledgements

To my daughter Patina Holman, without her support, I would still be working on this book. Thanks for assisting me in this endeavor. Thanks for typing and re-typing, she was my editor. Thanks, love you.

Thanks, Jennifer Frensley-Webb, for all of your support to my Outreach Ministries. You have been a blessing to me and so many here in Nashville.

I would be remiss if I did not thank all my friends that cheered me on to finish this edition. God bless you all.

A special thanks to Theresa Nichols who was God sent in my life, with her wisdom and knowledge, this dream has become a reality. I give God all the glory

Dorothy (Dot) Holman
Thankful

Through My Eyes

This book has been written to open our eyes to how trees and people are alike. I hope this book will let you see trees through my eyes and that this book will help you plant seeds in many lives throughout the world, also that these seeds will grow strong and tall like the trees for generations. May these seeds of wisdom and sunshine continue on and on in your lives and others for such a time as this.

Through My Eyes

My hope as well is that as you go through life's journey, you will see all the beautiful work that our God has done. Trees and humans are one of God's greatest masterpieces, with so many colors, sizes and shapes.

Trees and Humans are a twin win.

We need each other.

Grateful,
Dorothy (Dot) Holman

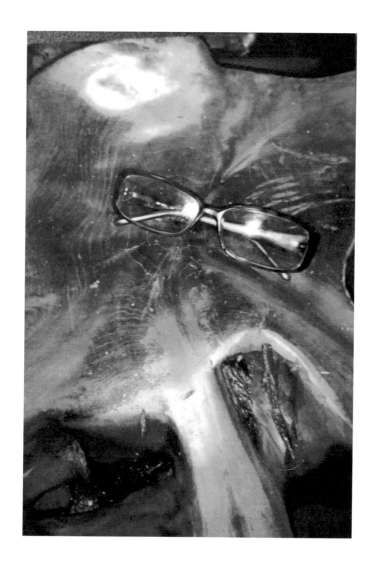

FROM THE SAME SOIL

This book will change your life and you will never look at trees the same on your life's journey.

There are many lessons to be learned from trees. Hundreds of different species can live together in the same community in peace.

Life lesson – so can we!

We have skin – so do trees.

We shed our skin – so do trees.

Dirt is the skin over the earth.

We go through seasons in our life.

Spring, summer, fall and winter – baby, youth, adult and super senior

Like trees, the wind comes, and the wind goes, but they still stand and with God we can stand as well.

The trees know in the winter season not to give up, better days are coming, if they just stand and never give up. "Life Lesson."

Philippians 4:13
I can do all things through Christ who strengthens me.

Trees/Humans

Some are Tall

Some are Short

Some are Small

Some come in different Shapes

Some come in different Sizes

Some come in different Colors, but they are still trees and humans. Some trees look just alike, but like twins, they are different.

FROM THE SAME SOIL

SEASONS

In the Fall, when all the leaves fall off, it shows the true colors of the tree and true character of them.

Some people are like trees, they come and they go, but true friends are like roots, they don't come and go.

LIFE

Humans can lose a leg, an eye or an arm, and we can still be beautiful. We can stand strong and go on through this journey called life with joy and peace.

OUR SEASONS

Baby-Youth-Adult-Old Age
Spring-Summer-Fall-Winter

Words are one of the most powerful things on earth. They can kill a spirit or they can heal a spirit. This book is to heal a spirit. This book is designed to bring joy, hope and encouragement. My hope is you will look at trees as a **Life Lesson** and that you will live out your gift and purpose.

Thank you, Lord.
Our prayers are the roots of our faith.

From William Whittakers

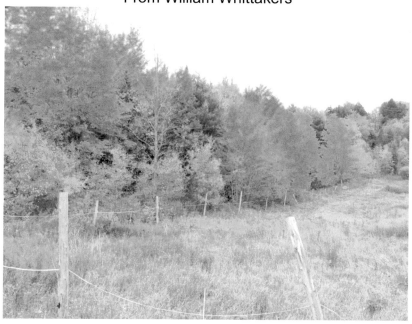

In the Beginning

FROM THE SAME SOIL

Genesis 1:11
Then God said "Let the earth bring forth grass, the herb that yields seed, and the fruit tree that yield fruit according to its kind. Whose seed is in itself, on the earth" and it was so.

Genesis 1:26
Then God said "Let Us make man in our image according to our likeness; let them have dominion over the fish of the sea, over the birds of the air, over the cattle, over all the earth and over every creeping thing on earth."

Trees/Humans

Trees are an echo of Life

These trees gave us a new beginning and a new ending to life's journey

DID YOU KNOW???

Trees were here before Christ walked on the earth.

DO YOU KNOW???

How many trees are in the world?

DO YOU KNOW???

How many humans are in the world?

It's true that trees were here before humans and they both came from the same soil. No one really knows how many trees or humans are in the world.

Google said "That the world is home to over three trillion trees. There are over 400 trees to each human.

No one really knows exactly when Jesus was born. Some scholars think He was born between 6 B. C. and 4 B. C. based purely on the Biblical story of Herod the Great. **Luke 2:1-7** and it came to pass in those days, that there went out a decree from Caesar Augustus, that all the world should be taxed.

Thanks for going on this journey.

Thanks, Jeff Neal, for these beautiful trees.

STILL DOING GOOD ANYWAY

Sometimes trees and humans don't look like we think they should look, but it does not stop the trees and humans from doing what they were created to do in their lifetime. Some trees, regardless of how they look, still produce beautiful leaves, they also provide housing for different kinds of birds and other animals. If you look beyond how the tree looks, you will see the tree living out its purpose. Some humans don't look like Hollywood, but they don't let their looks stop them from living out their God given purpose.

When a tree goes through the coldest winter, it knows that better days are coming. Humans don't know how strong they are until being strong is the only choice they have. Trees, like humans, are one of God's most beautiful amazing works.

NEVER GIVE UP

Fell years ago.
Never gave up.

A tree can fall down, but keeps growing for years to come.

Humans fall down, but they get back up and keep growing.

Some trees are moved to different places, but they keep growing.

Sometimes we have to move and life changes, but like trees, we can also keep growing where we are planted.

Life Lesson

No matter how low we get in life, we can get back up again. A sinner can become a saint when we get back up.

LOOK ALIKE, BUT DIFFERENT

There are trees that look just alike, but they are different.

Twins look alike, but they are different as well. Families are like branches and roots on trees. Humans grow like branches and roots and we grow different and yet our roots remain as one. The roots of our generation can go for years.

Jesus said "Abide in me and I in you. As the branch cannot bear fruit of itself, unless it abides in the vine neither can you unless you abide in me." (John 15:4)

"I am the vine you are the branches. He who abides in me, and I in him bears much fruit; for without me you can do nothing."

TREES/HUMANS

23

BEAUTIFUL DIFFERENT, BUT STILL ALIKE

PLANTED BY WATER

PSALMS 1:3

LIKE A TREE PLANTED BY WATER

HOUSING, FOOD AND SHADE

Trees provide homes for the homeless, as well as food for the homeless, birds of the air and other creeping things.

Trees are moved to different places, but they keep growing. They grow where they are planted. **Life Lesson**.

Humans are living organisms. A tree's roots are the life line to the trees, our prayers are the roots of our faith.

Wisdom is a seed and it will grow like a tree within us.

THROUGH IT ALL

THROUGH SPRING, SUMMER, FALL AND WINTER
STILL STANDING BETTER DAYS

Thank you, Lord, our prayers are the root of our faith. May the roots go deep into the soil of God's love for all he has done.

Thank you, Lord, that you can keep us standing through it all, even when we are leaning, you are there.

If you stand for something, be prepared to stand alone like a tree and if you fall on the ground, fall like a seed that grows back and never gives up.

A tree can fall down, but keeps growing for years to come.

We fall down in life, but we get back up again and keep growing. **Life Lesson**.

THE TREE COMMUNITY

THEY LIVE IN PEACE

LIFE LESSON

Sisters and brothers grow in different directions, but it does not change the fact that they are still sisters and brothers.

I AM DIFFERENT, BUT I STILL HAVE PURPOSE

LOOK PERFECT

WITHIN

Some trees look so perfect, but you can't see what's going on inside. We humans are the same way.

Some humans look perfect on the outside, sometimes they are so broken on the inside, they commit suicide. Like the trees that fall, but look so perfect from the outside, we can stand with Jesus' help.

Some trees just bend with wind but don't break, we bend with life's problems, but we don't break as well with Jesus' help.

This tree looked good on the outside but this big branch fell from the tree, like humans look good on the outside, but broken on the inside.

WE STILL HAVE PURPOSE

REGARDLESS OF HOW WE MAY LOOK

TREES/HUMANS

Did you know that trees were the first AC system for the earth and for people? Humans invented the AC system much later. Willis Carrier invented the air conditioner in 1902. Save the trees, save us!

Tree roots are like the human body's nervous system. They both transmit signals. Without these signals, the trees and the human body cannot live. Life Lessons.

NEVER CHANGE

Some trees never change they stay green all year. Some people never change their character and attitude stays the same year in and year out. They need the peace of Jesus. Like a green tree a good friend never changes. Like a mother's love, it never changes.

LIFE LESSON

JUST STAND

Storms are a part of life, trees understand that and humans they have to have strong faith and know that everything works together for good, for those that love the Lord and behind those dark clouds there are blue skies and sunshine. If we just stand.

LIFE LESSON

HUMANS/TREES

FROM THE SAME SOIL

All trees are beautiful.

All humans are beautiful.

It's not how we look at things in life, but how we see them.

The mustard seed is so very small, but inside of it is great potential.

THE MUSTARD SEED

Matthew 17:20
So, Jesus said to them "Because of your unbelief, assuredly, I say to you, if you have faith as a mustard seed, you will say to this mountain move from here to there, and it will move from here to there and it will move, and nothing will be impossible for you."

"However, this kind does not go out except by prayer and fasting."

Matthew 13:31-32

31 Another parable put he forth unto them, saying, The kingdom of heaven is like to a grain of mustard seed, which a man took, and sowed in his field:

32 Which indeed is the least of all seeds: but when it is grown, it is the greatest among herbs, and becometh a tree, so that the birds of the air come and lodge in the branches thereof.

REPRODUCTION

The reproduction of trees and humans both come from a small seed. The reproduction of our food comes from trees and farmers.

All of the great trees started as a seed.

THE MUSTARD SEED

Mustard Trees grow in abundance beside the Sea of Galilee and in the southern hill country of Judea on the Mount of Olives. These trees are not individually planted by local farmers, but by birds and the winds carrying their seeds and scattering them about. Once rooted, the trees grow to heights of eight to twelve feet. In the springtime, these colorful yellow plants are found with birds nesting among their branches.

Jesus taught that the Kingdom of God is like both the tiny mustard seed and the full-grown mustard tree. Small or large, God's providential care is there for its growth. To Jesus' listeners, the mustard seed symbolized something small and apparently lifeless. Yet they know when it was sown, it would spring life as a full, grown tree. In another parable, Jesus said "Unless a grain of wheat falls into the ground and dies, it remains alone, but if it dies, it produces much grain." (John 12:24). Paul also drew from this teaching when he said, "This mortal has put on immortality (1st Corinthians 15:54). So then, a seed and the death of the seed, brings forth life and renewed faith.

We can be confident that out of the tiniest of possibilities, God will raise and establish His Kingdom. Out of our little beginnings,

He will reap a full harvest. Whether you have a great task, or a small responsibility, do it joyfully, for out of your endeavors, God will raise bountiful blessings. Remember, anyone can count the seeds in an apple, but only God can count the apples in a seed!

SAVE THE TREES, SAVE US

The world is the home to over 60 trillion of tree species and trillion of trees on earth is the best estimate. No man knows how many trees there are on the earth. They have estimated that there are 7.53 billion people in the world. No one knows for the soil as well.

Genesis 5 numbers are in tenths of years which explains how it reads 930 years for 93 for Adam and 969 years for Methuselah instead of 96 and Noah 950 instead of 95.

The human race used to live a longer life before the body got defiled by chemicals, foods with pesticides, medicines and other toxins. Trees are being defiled by toxins, they are being cut down and burned down by manmade fires, etc....

HELP SAVE US - FROM THE SAME SOIL

TREES IN THE BEGINNING AND TREES IN THE END

Revelations 22:14

"That they may have the right to the Tree of Life"

It's true that trees were here before humans and they both came from the soil. My hope and intention are to broaden your knowledge on how much alike trees and humans are.

The Redwood tree holds the title for the tallest tree, but not the oldest. The Bristlecone Pine tree lives longer than the Redwood, with oldest one approximately 5,000 years old.

Trees in the beginning and trees in the end. It's true that trees were here before humans and both came from the soil.

All trees came with a purpose. All humans have a purpose in their lifetime.

All trees are different, but still alike.

All people are different, but still alike.

Bristlecone Pine

Redwood trees below

Remember, we all can live together in peace and love.

Leviticus 19:18 "Love your neighbor as yourself."

Thanks for going on this journey with me.

WE ARE ALIKE TREES AND HUMANS

Dorothy (Dot) Holman

FROM THE SAME SOIL

I hope you have enjoyed this journey through my eyes of some of life's lessons. I hope you will go with me through my second edition *From the Same Soil* coming soon.

Thanks, and may God's favor be with you,

Dorothy (Dot) Holman

About the Author

Dorothy (Dot) Holman

Affiliations Past and Present

Metro Reautification Bureau Board Member

Bethlehem Centers of Nashville Board Member

Baptist Sunday School Board Project Director

International Service Systems Human Resource Director

Margaret Maddox Family YMCA Property Services and Senior Adult Director

TN School Board Association Coordinator of Property Services

Founded the Margaret Maddox YMCA Bible Ministry (at present over 5,000 Bibles have been distributed)

John Henry Hale Mini Park Founder and Coordinator

Founder and Coordinator of Future Club for Pre-teens and Teens at John Henry Hale Homes

Metro Schools Motivational Speaker for High School Kids

President of the Missionary Society at Jackson Street Missionary Baptist Church – Curtis Bryant Pastor

Founder and Coordinator of The Helping Hands Ministry at Crystal Fountain Church – Rev. Dr. Michael V. Graves

FROM THE SAME SOIL

Founder and Coordinator of The Ambassador Club Outreach Ministry at The Margaret Maddox YMCA

Small Business Owner

Dot's Janitorial Services

Founded God's Love Ministries (45 years of service Outreach in the Nashville Community)

Free Bibles, books and other acts of love

Worked with Agencies

Metro Government Agencies to better Nashville Communities

Mayor Richard Fulton

Ann Chapman-Metro Beautification Bureau

Councilman Ludey Wallace

Councilman John Cooper

Councilman Brent Withers

My 2017-2018 Goals

Dear Crossing Signs on Riverside Drive

Mini Libraries for the Homeless Shelters (First 3 already in place – New Beginnings Church and Homeless Shelter for Ladies, Carl R. Horton, Pastor)

1. Matthew 25 Residence for Homeless Men
2. East Nashville Cooperative Ministry

Supporting My Ministries

Bob Frensley Chrysler Jeep Dealership – Jennifer Frensley Webb

1st and 2nd Chance Furniture Mattresses – Robert Holt

A host of family and friends

Save-A-Lot Management

H. G. Hills – Management

Awards
Receiving Proclamation from Brenda Gilmore from Tennessee State Senate

The people in the picture are my grandson, Brandon Holman, daughter, Patina Holman, son Bobby Holman, and Tennessee State Senate Brenda Gilmore and Pastor Michael Graves

Some pictures of the Mini Libraries

East Nashville Coop Ministries

Matthew 25 for Homeless Men's Mission

Purse donations from New Beginning Missionary Baptist Church for women coming out of prison starting a new life trained by loving volunteers

Certificates

The YMCA group that I started (Ambassadors' Club)
I had them doing all kinds of outreach. This was a volunteer
outreach group.

Recognition from the House of Representatives

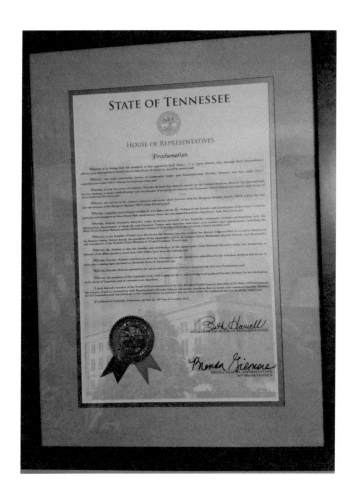

Recognition from the House of Representatives

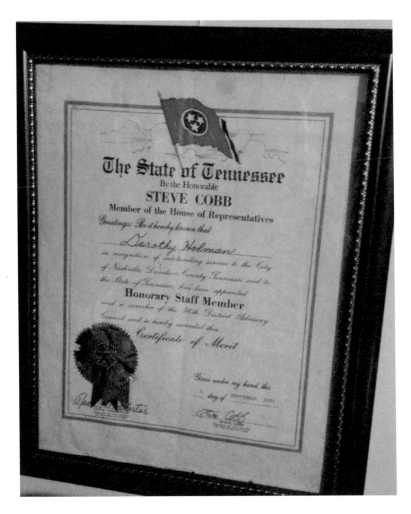

Mayor Fulton of Nashville

A member of Jackson Street Missionary Baptist Church, Robert L. Pearson, Pastor

FROM THE SAME SOIL

Photos of front yard

My front yard and my neighbor's with wild turkeys taking over. LOL

FROM THE SAME SOIL

Your donations for this book will help me help others.

"May God's love be with each reader."

Contact information:
Dorothyholman50@yahoo.com
615-474-1925

ISBN: 9781096339144

Made in the USA
Columbia, SC
06 January 2024

29520773R00042